9 QUALITIES OF AN EFFECTIVE LEADER

What They Know and Do!

Jerrund Wilkerson, PD, MBA, PCC

WESTBOW
PRESS®
A DIVISION OF THOMAS NELSON
& ZONDERVAN

WestBow Press books may be ordered through
booksellers or by contacting:

WestBow Press
A Division of Thomas Nelson & Zondervan
1663 Liberty Drive
Bloomington, IN 47403
www.westbowpress.com
844-714-3454

Scriptures taken from the Holy Bible, New International Version®, NIV®.
Copyright © 1973, 1978, 1984, 2011 by Biblica, Inc.™ Used by permission
of Zondervan. All rights reserved worldwide. www.zondervan.com
The "NIV" and "New International Version" are trademarks registered
in the United States Patent and Trademark Office by Biblica, Inc.®

ISBN: 978-1-6642-8079-3 (sc)
ISBN: 978-1-6642-8078-6 (e)

Print information available on the last page.

WestBow Press rev. date: 11/16/2022

Dedicated To:

Kacee, Lauren (Lolly), Jay(Bud), Brad, Cliff, Ms. Riley,
BJ, Parker(Toostie Roll), Macen(Bop) & Charlie.

SAWUBONA

Contents

Vision

Clarity about what your mission is and why you're on it.

- ➤ Effective leaders always start with a compelling vision of an achievable and better future.

- ➤ Effective leaders know to trust their gut. Their minds are powerful tools, and they don't allow others to sway them from their vision before all the needed research and planning is done for a way forward.

- ➤ Effective leaders know each day is a gift. Realizing yesterday is gone and tomorrow is not here yet, they strive to make the most of every opportunity *today*.

- ➤ Effective leaders know visioning is important for betterment. This is the *what*; however, they also know followers generally need to know the *how* before they become fully engaged.

- ➤ Effective leaders know that having vision is important; however, they also know a key ingredient for positive outcomes is inspiration. Leaders must create cultures and systems to inspire their followers.

- ➤ Effective leaders know the value of visioning. They work from the principle that if the mind can conceive it, they can achieve it.

➤ Effective leaders know the value of visualizing. They can put themselves in the endgame before it happens.

➤ Effective leaders know they need to set aside time to reflect on achievements and set future-forward goals.

➤ Effective leaders know adding talent to their teams is an ongoing process. They are continually on the lookout for top talent, internally and externally.

➤ Effective leaders know how to segment the vision into bite-size pieces, providing short- and long-term outcomes and highlighting how everyone fits into the vision.

➤ As highlighted by DISC® research, effective leaders know that, in order to achieve effective outcomes, they are grounded with the foundation of vision, inspiration, alignment, and execution.

➤ Effective leaders know and embrace the childhood story *The Little Engine That Could,* which highlights the mindset of effective leaders: "If you think you can, you can!"

➤ Effective leaders know those who don't take chances don't make advances.

➢ Effective leaders know opportunities can disguise themselves as problems.

➢ To be relevant, effective leaders maintain an internal organizational focus while being aware of their external landscape.

➢ Effective leaders set examples of the changes they want to see.

➢ While outcome dots cannot be connected until after the action has been done, effective leaders work toward a vision in which actions are taken to make sure all dots are connected during the process.

➢ Effective leaders know one of their key responsibilities is to be vision communicators to their followers.

➢ Effective leaders know criticism is part of their journey. If the leader is saying or doing things that matter, they know some people will not like the changes being driven.

➢ Effective leaders are often *what-if* individuals.

➢ Effective leaders are guided by optimism, can-do attitudes, and expectations of winning.

- Effective leaders know success always starts with a positive attitude. They know that attitude determines altitude.

- Effective leaders don't see challenges or problems, but only opportunities in disguise.

- Effective leaders know circumstances create opportunities.

- Effective leaders know circumstances are often created by their choices.

- Effective leaders know results are only limited by their imaginations.

- Effective leaders know they must see around corners so they can anticipate needs and *respond* rather than react!

- Effective leaders know to encourage innovation and not fear failure.

- Effective leaders know they will not always hit their targets or make things work the first time around; however, they know they must at least try, recalibrate as needed, and try again for worthy causes.

➢ Effective leaders know happiness does not come from the outside (external environment) but rather starts from within.

➢ Effective leaders know the future does not just happen by chance, but is shaped by decisions. Therefore, effective leaders must consistently keep their end goals in mind.

Influence

Positive influence sparks motivation and engagement.

➢ While this is a challenging balance, effective leaders know they cannot both submerge themselves into the group and lead the group at the same time.

➢ Effective leaders know leading will be a challenge at times and that criticism will be inevitable. However, effective leaders always consider the source when their focus is being critiqued.

➢ Effective leaders know they should be other-oriented. They consistently and intentionally seek ways to add value to others, especially those within their inner circle.

➢ Effective leaders know the difference between a group of followers and a team of followers. Considering individuals' strengths, the leader consistently strives to create a team approach, aligning strengths with tasks and responsibilities to produce focused and coordinated outcomes.

➢ Effective leaders know they must be self-aware and lead themselves before they can effectively lead and develop others.

➤ Effective leaders know the people they spend the most time with often influence them the most.

➤ Since each person is different and has value, effective leaders know listening to and following their instincts is a key to being or becoming purpose-driven; therefore, effective leaders become more intentional about what they do, why they do it, and how they do it.

➤ Effective leaders know their people want to know they matter to the leader; therefore, effective leaders know they must touch hearts before they can ask for helping hands.

➤ Effective leaders know they need to set the examples they expect to see. They know people's behaviors and subsequent actions are based on what they see more than what they hear or read.

➤ Effective leaders know they must strive to give more than they receive.

➤ Effective leaders give more than they take and don't keep score.

➤ Effective leaders respect and care about their followers; therefore, they invest time and resources.

➢ Effective leaders know the difference between leading and managing. Processes are managed; however, people are led. An effective leader can be a manager; however, an effective manager is not necessarily a leader.

➢ Effective leaders inspire followers to take intelligent, committed actions toward a predetermined goal.

➢ Effective leaders know they will always be effective leaders regardless of their fields of endeavor.

➢ Realizing no one player should stop the show, effective leaders know they should always seek to duplicate themselves through intentional bench-strength development. They have backups.

➢ Effective leaders know, like good athletes, the quality of your leadership shows in the outcomes of your production and achievements.

➢ Effective leaders know they don't need to show their leadership badges; their influence speaks loudly.

➢ Effective leaders know their effectiveness is measured by being able to identify and mobilize others to produce beneficial outcomes in a constantly changing environment.

➤ Effective leaders understand the bottom lines of all their efforts are focused on not just transactions for the moment, but also transformation for the long term.

➤ Effective leaders know how to tell stories that convey their messages and visions and inspire others to follow.

➤ While commanding facts and competence is very important, effective leaders know people need emotion injections to be inspired enough to remain committed followers.

➤ *Why* is the key and central ingredient effective leaders focus on to inspire followership.

➤ Effective leaders know that winning is a learned habit. Unfortunately, so is losing.

➤ Effective leaders build other leaders intentionally, routinely, and systematically to ensure success is sustained.

➤ Effective leaders know one bad apple can spoil the whole barrel of good apples; therefore, they remove the bad apple to preserve the continuity and quality of the good ones.

➢ Effective leaders know they must duplicate themselves; however, surrounding themselves with individuals who share their values is critical for coordinated and continual growth.

➢ Washington Irving once wrote, "Great minds have purpose; others have wishes." Effective leaders know that purpose breeds hope and hope gives strength and courage needed to keep moving forward.

➢ Effective leaders know they need to manage things and processes but lead people.

➢ Effective leaders know to align with Peter F. Drucker and the eight leadership practices he highlighted:

    o Identify what needs to be done.

    o Identify what is best for the enterprise.

    o Develop action plans.

    o Take responsibility for decisions.

    o Take responsibility for communication.

    o Focus on opportunities rather than problems.

    o Run productive meetings.

o Think and say "we" rather than "I."

➢ Effective leaders know the distinction between management and leadership:

    o Management involves planning and budgeting. Leadership involves setting direction.

    o Management involves organizing and staffing. Leadership involves aligning people.

    o Management provides controls and solves problems. Leadership helps create motivation by inspiration.

➢ Some leaders believe in rewarding all followers, no matter what. Effective leaders know to value all followers and praise efforts; however, they only reward goal-oriented performances and real achievements.

➢ Effective leaders know they need to manage things and processes but lead people.

➢ Effective leaders know that in order to create other leaders, they must identify and intentionally create opportunities for potential leaders to spread their wings and grow.

➤ Effective leaders know delegation is a key way to develop leadership.

➤ Since effective leaders are always about growth and progress that result in change, they approach all situations with a healthy dose of optimism while also listening to followers who have opposing views.

➤ Effective leaders know they must strike the delicate balance between helping followers see and feel the need for change while not feeling overwhelmed by the change.

➤ Effective leaders know and understand change is challenging. Followers can only focus on and implement one change at a time.

➤ Effective leaders agree with coach Jimmy Johnson: "Treat a person as he is and he will remain as he is. Treat him as what he could be and he will become what he should be."

➤ Effective leaders know followers are gained when the leader is valued and respected.

➤ Effective leaders know they are the sum total of their followers, so they intentionally work to positively support and equip their circles of influence.

➤ Effective leaders know a word of praise or a sincere thank-you is often worth more than money.

➤ Effective leaders know history is *history*—it's in the past. They use the past, not as a roadblock to success, but rather as a guidepost to navigate a better future outcome.

➤ Effective leaders know their primary job is to give followers hope, inspiring within them a reason for being.

➤ Effective leaders know book smarts (IQ) are important however, they also know emotional smarts (EQ) are even more important when connecting with people for results and overall impact.

➤ Effective leaders know people buy into people first before they buy an idea or product.

➤ Effective leaders know the best followers are those who not only want to be successful, but also want to be significant. Success is individually focused however, significance is also about including others.

➤ Effective leaders reflect on what they desire and mirror what they admire.

➢ Effective leaders understand and embrace the saying, "Show me your friends and I'll show you your future!"

➢ Effective leaders know the importance of establishing daily priorities and goals to be achieved.

Engagement

3

Remain grounded in the realities of the business in order to inspire the team to unleash their passion and talents around the shared vision.

➢ Effective leaders know bias can be disruptive to a team.

➢ Effective leaders communicate often and consistently, highlighting what finished looks like.

➢ Effective leaders know that, while ongoing engagement with followers is important, intentionally creating quality time with their families is equally important. Sometimes they must make reservations.

➢ Effective leaders know the importance of delegation. They understand the need to develop their teams for success versus being a one-person show.

➢ Effective leaders know they need teams of followers to achieve best results; therefore, they intentionally surround themselves with individuals who possess complimentary talents and skills and encourage their engagement toward the goal or vision.

➢ Effective leaders know a healthy home life is important. Family tends to consist of the people who know them best and provide unconditional love. Touching base regularly with loved ones can help leaders and team members alike stay grounded.

➤ Since who we spend time with shapes and influences who we are, effective leaders know they need to be positively surrounded. They intentionally surround themselves with positive influences, or as American author Shawn Achor calls them, *pillars*, *bridges* or *connectors*, and *extenders*.

➤ Effective leaders measure personal impact by the number of people they serve rather than the number of people who serve them.

➤ Effective leaders know that when their work is done, their followers will say "we" achieved it.

➤ Effective leaders know that to have sustained engagement and support, their followers must find a sense of purpose and meaning in what the leader presents.

➤ Effective leaders see value in each follower and strive to engage on individual levels.

➤ Effective leaders know inspired teams are high-performing teams, so they work to create an environment in which the best team members choose to stay on their team, even when they have other options.

➤ Effective leaders know money is not always the best incentive for their followers. Their rewards are relevant to the team and culture.

➤ Effective leaders know their own strengths and leverage them effectively. They are also aware of their weaknesses and find team members who fill those gaps.

➤ Effective leaders respect each follower and intentionally engage each in accordance with his or her individual value and contribution to the vision.

➤ Effective leaders know ongoing connections with their followers is very important. Social media and digital technology have introduced new avenues of connection. Effective leaders know to continually keep their fingers on the pulse of all avenues of communication in order to keep their followers engaged.

➤ Effective leaders understand the need for two-way engagement between themselves and their followers. Leaders should express clearly what's needed from a follower while also listening to the follower's needs. This way, they're able to maintain mutually beneficial relationships.

➤ Effective leaders know it's not all about who they are as individuals. Collaborating with their teams provides them with eyes, arms, and legs for complete views and approaches.

➤ Effective leaders embrace the admonition of Zig Zeiglar: "Your attitude determines your altitude."

➤ Effective leaders know the Arab proverb: "An army of sleep led by a lion would defeat an army of lions led by a sheep.

➤ Effective leaders know they cannot grow, transform, or build a team by doing the work for others. Each person must carry his or her own weight. Ken Blanchard highlighted this point in his book, _The One Minute Manager Meets the Monkey._

➤ Effective leaders know that in order to achieve sustained success, they must see with both eyes. They keep one eye on their team (the internal environment) and the other eye on the external environment.

➤ People might listen to what you say however, effective leaders know their actions speak louder than words.

- ➤ Effective leaders have extensive and robust networks, both internally and externally.

- ➤ Effective leaders know that while vision and plan-clarity are important, the heartbeat of a team's top performance is execution.

- ➤ Effective leaders know they cannot motivate individuals because motivation is internal) however, they can and must inspire those around them.

- ➤ While passion is important, effective leaders know having purpose is the real driver, because purpose provides meaning. Effective leaders always want to help followers engage by explaining why.

- ➤ Effective leaders know they must fully touch their followers' hearts before they can ask for helping hands (get full engagement and execution).

- ➤ Effective leaders understand that *knowing* does not necessarily translate to *growing*. Action must follow knowledge for growth.

- ➤ Effective leaders know that success is nothing more than having clear goals associated with a few disciplines practiced every day until they're achieved.

- Effective leaders know they should strive to be like ginger ale—a good mixer with everything.

- Effective leaders know rapport is basic for positive social connections. Building rapport through eye contact is key.

- Effective leaders know the prophetic words of Frederick Douglass are true: "If there is no struggle, there is no progress."

- Effective leaders know they must build strong relationships and also know they must choose them wisely and intentionally.

- Effective leaders know passion and *stick-to-itiveness* will make an impact. Starbucks' CEO Howard Schultz said it best: "When you're surrounded by people who share a passionate commitment around a common purpose, anything is possible."

- Effective leaders know there is no *I* in team. *I* is replaced with *we*.

- Effective leaders know how to embrace this thought from Jim Rohm: "The unique combination of desire, planning, effort, and perseverance will always work its magic. The question is not whether the formula for success will work for a person but whether a person will work the formula?"

➢ Effective leaders know two of the most powerful word combinations are *not* "I kinda" or "I might" or "I hope," but "I *will*"!

➢ Effective leaders know that if their followers are afraid of them, it will kill candor and guarantee performances will be below potential and/or expectations.

➢ Effective leaders know they must replace programs, products, initiatives, and even people, who have outlived their usefulness.

➢ Effective leaders know they must get out of their stations and interact face-to-face with followers in the followers' respective stations.

➢ Effective leaders know collaboration is the precursor to innovation

➢ Effective leaders know they must write down goals to be most effective in achieving them.

➢ Effective leaders know the importance of delegation.

➢ Effective leaders know change happens at the speed of trust.

Communication

Communication fosters alignment and execution.

➢ Effective leaders know they must be trustworthy, build relationships, and communicate well to maintain their effectiveness.

➢ Effective leaders know that how an individual responds to adversity is what separates someone ordinary from an extraordinary achiever.

➢ Effective leaders know the importance of ongoing and frequent communication updates with followers to ensure their engagement and support. Info is shared about the mission and what is going well, as well as areas for improvement.

➢ Effective leaders know they must have plans to formally meet with all their followers and discuss progress on preestablished KPIs (key performance indicators).

➢ Effective leaders know acknowledging jobs well done to followers is often more appreciated and valued than money.

➢ Effective leaders know fuzzy communication of expectations will produce fuzzy outcomes.

➢ Effective leaders know to give specific feedback (task and behavioral) regularly and thoughtfully.

➤ Effective leaders know major outcome disappointments are the results of failure to set clear expectations and/or having the wrong people in positions of responsibility.

➤ Effective leaders know many followers need to understand not just the whys, but the hows of initiatives, so leaders must clarify what success looks and feels like.

➤ When delivering potentially challenging feedback, effective leaders know to express concerns about the situational outcomes and *not* attack individuals.

➤ Effective leaders know not to leave their followers in suspense. Striving to remove or at least minimize ambiguity, they are clear and direct communicators.

➤ Effective leaders know the importance of celebrating the little victories as well as big wins.

➤ Effective leaders know to continually keep the vision in front of the followers as well as the progress being made.

➤ Effective leaders know to create traditions that celebrate their values.

- ➢ Effective leaders always clarify current reality before focusing on the vision of hope and future forward. They work from here and now with an eye on the horizon. Dr. Martin Luther King inspired and mobilized his followers and a nation with this approach.

- ➢ Effective leaders know to appeal to their followers' *heads* and *hearts* for full engagement.

- ➢ Since effective leaders know they have two ears and one mouth, listening is critical. They listen twice as much as they talk.

- ➢ Effective leaders know just being good enough is the enemy of striving for excellence.

- ➢ Effective leaders know they must be very good listeners. There are always upper stories (what is shared) and lower stories (what is meant).

- ➢ Effective leaders know that in order to captivate people, they must be excellent communicators.

- ➢ Effective leaders know that visibility and being present are important. Emailing, texting, posting, and so forth are only supplemental tools.

➢ Effective leaders know the future doesn't just happen. It is influenced and shaped by prior decisions made. Therefore, effective leaders must consistently keep their end goals in mind.

➢ Effective leaders know the value of listening twice as much as talking.

Problem Solving

This is a continuous activity and actually shows the value of the leader. Problems are constant and so must be the focus and efforts of the leader to resolve or minimize them.

> ➤ Effective leaders know that when they see gaps in their teams' performances, the first close look should be at themselves.

> ➤ Effective leaders are not excuse people, but rather can do people. Effective leaders know there will always be hurdles when they strive to achieve visions; however, rather than see hurdles as problems or excuses not to proceed, they remain focused and persist until they overcome the hurdles.

> ➤ Effective leaders know to do first things first and ensuring culture and talent development are in place first. Effective leaders begin their day by setting things in motion around their agenda (vision and goals) *first* before becoming a part of someone else's agenda (i.e., checking text, email, phone calls, and so forth).

> ➤ Effective leaders know their main missions are to:

> > o Build and ensure a strong, positive culture is in place and

o Talent development is aligned with culture, on-going.

➤ Effective leaders know to follow the teaching of William Arthur Ward: "Begin while others are procrastinating and work while others are wishing."

➤ Effective leaders know to follow the five Ps principle for guidance: *Prior Planning Prevents Poor Performance.*

➤ Effective leaders know processes must be created and implemented to get things done smoothly and efficiently.

➤ Effective leaders know being a problem solver is a key trait for them and their followers.

➤ Effective leaders know sometimes talking through issues or challenges can be valuable.

➤ Effective leaders make people moves quickly. They know the faster they place the best people in the best positions for success, the faster positive outcomes will be achieved.

➤ Effective leaders know to set clear and specific achievement expectations *at the beginning* of a project.

- ➢ Effective leaders know the goal of all feedback is always to make things better.

- ➢ Effective leaders know to address problems quickly.

- ➢ Effective leaders know working from a principle-based foundation is important and also know they must applaud and challenge their followers based on where the followers are.

- ➢ Effective leaders intentionally select and design their teams so that key positions, and subsequently individuals, are chosen to support the leader's vision and expected outcomes.

- ➢ When choosing team members, effective leaders know how to choose wisely. They know the qualities and traits they're looking for and compare prospects accordingly. Past performances and behaviors are strong indicators of future performances and behaviors.

- ➢ Effective leaders know when adding followers to their team, they need to engage other interviewers and seek trusted recommendations to help close the selection loop.

- ➢ Effective leaders know to take the long view when adding to their team. They select individuals who are capable of more than just their current job.

➤ Effective leaders know top talent is hard to find and keep, so they intentionally and continually survey environments. They keep a pulse on both climates and make engaging adjustments as needed to create and inspire team wholeness.

➤ Effective leaders know the importance of making themselves available to their followers i.e. for face-to-face communication.

➤ Effective leaders know many competing stimuli can distract followers, so the leader ensures followers focus on priorities within time frame expectations for progress.

➤ While all followers have value and are important, effective leaders understand the 80/20 rule and prioritize focused time accordingly.

➤ Since connecting with stakeholders is important, effective leaders know to talk with them to set the standard for clarity and expectations.

➤ Effective leaders know to connect with followers on the level of "what's in it for them" (WIIFM) as well as how the leader's vision impacts the future.

➤ While social media has its place in the communication process, effective leaders know face-to-face communication is still the most effective way to negotiate mutually beneficial outcomes and ways forward.

➤ Since leadership is about change and change can be uncomfortable or challenging for some, effective leaders know to test the waters by conducting pilot engagements before revealing changes that affect all followers.

➤ Effective leaders know to track both qualitative and quantitative metrics and keep score, because their efforts are always toward measurable results and outcomes.

➤ After all is said and done, often more is said than done. Effective leaders know talking and activity must be focused on measurable results to achieve progress.

➤ Effective leaders know not everything that appears to be urgent is necessarily important.

➤ Effective leaders know talk is cheap. They value followers who do.

➤ Doing things rather than just thinking about them is a hallmark trait of an effective leader.

- Effective leaders know the bigger the challenge, the more enthusiasm is needed!

- Effective leaders know all problems and challenges they encounter introduce them to themselves for a reaction or response.

- Effective leaders understand the need and how to be strategic. They know what's best to do among the things competing for their attention and how to get them done.

- Effective leaders know not to major in minors. In other words, they are not known for doing insignificant or wrong things well.

- Effective leaders don't wait to dot every "i" and cross every "t" before they make a decision.

- Effective leaders know the significant difference between accomplishments and achievements. In other words, they know the difference between activity and progress.

- Effective leaders understand: Do what's easy and life will be hard. Do what's hard and life will be easy!

- Effective leaders hear what individuals say; however, they pay more attention to what the individual does. They know past behaviors are relatively good predictors of future behaviors and performances.

➢ Effective leaders understand the reality that needs determine their schedules rather than the convenience of time.

➢ Effective leaders know if they cannot change things around them, they change things around them.

➢ Effective leaders know they must approach each situation as if standing on a balcony looking at changes from a 360 degree view. They consider all stakeholders and realize all actions have consequences on the outcome.

➢ Effective leaders know multiple changes at once will cause frustration and/or disorientation in followers who are expected to implement changes.

➢ Effective leaders understand: "To know and not do is not yet to know" (Zen saying)

➢ Effective leaders know they don't know it all. So they surround themselves with others who help them see 360 degrees to achieve success. Accountability buddies can make the road to success not only easier as well as more enjoyable.

- Effective leaders know they must always think ahead to make the most of every opportunity.

- Effective leaders know they are problem solvers. They don't complain, but rather approach each hurdle as an opportunity to show value and/or move the status quo.

- Effective leaders know to follow the guidance principle offered by Stephen Covey and highlighted in his book, *7 Habits of Highly Effective People*, and they begin with the end in mind. They may have to back into the process to achieve their targeted outcomes.

- Effective leaders know arrogance and pride come before a fall. Regardless of how sharp or talented the leaders are, they heed the admonition of King Solomon: "Plans fail for lack of counsel but with many advisors they succeed" (Proverbs 15:22 NIV). So they reach out.

- Effective leaders know one of the biggest obstacles to progress is indecision. Effective leaders are decisive and have a sense of urgency.

- Effective leaders know being good is *not* good enough when better is expected. Excellence is always the mindset.

➤ Effective leaders know the same minds or mindset that created the problem cannot fix the problem. They must gather new minds around the table to bring fresh perspectives.

➤ Effective leaders know they must remain focused on their goals until they are achieved or abandoned.

➤ Effective leaders set their own daily agendas first before checking emails, Facebook, or Twitter, where they could potentially become a part of someone else's agenda.

➤ Effective leaders know not to allow themselves to get tangled or lost in the weeds of a situation.

➤ Effective leaders know to start their day by accomplishing a simple task so as to set a productive tone of achievement for the remainder of the day. It can be something as simple as making your bed well upon rising.

Integrity

6

With integrity, effective leaders build strong relationships, create authenticity, engender trust, and drives higher levels of performance.

> ➤ Effective leaders know that trust and integrity are key bedrocks of their effectiveness foundations.

> ➤ Effective leaders know to avoid narcissistic thinking and behavior. They know all that glitters ain't gold, and followers will eventually see the glitter lose its luster.

> ➤ Effective leaders know that *trust* is the bedrock to gain follower's continued engagement and support. It is hard to regain if ever lost.

> ➤ Effective leaders see and embrace the *truth!*

> ➤ Effective leaders know nothing speaks louder about a person than their demonstrated and witnessed *character!!*

> ➤ Effective leaders know their conduct and actions are on display as an example to be emulated by followers.

> ➤ Effective leaders don't set out to lead, but rather to make a positive difference regarding a situation or circumstance.

➤ Effective leaders know there are times when hard conversations are needed and they deliver them.

➤ Effective leaders know *trust* is the most important ingredient for a leader; both in the leader and among the followers.

➤ Effective leaders are honest and transparent at the individual and group levels about performance relative to their missions and goals—no spin.

➤ Effective leaders do not tolerate dishonesty, bullying or dissension among followers.

➤ Effective leaders know being decisive is important, and they are clear and squarely own the decisions they make.

➤ Effective leaders know, because they are in a position of authority, their followers will not always tell them the unvarnished truth. So they must create environments where truth-telling is welcomed—and maybe even rewarded.

➤ Effective leaders know they must always walk their talk.

- ➢ Effective leaders know to be real. They are not actors or imposters. What you see is what you get.

- ➢ Effective leaders know when they operate from bases of authenticity, they are naturally centered and more trusted. Trust is foundational for ongoing followership.

- ➢ Effective leaders know they must always work from core values and authenticity.

- ➢ Trust is a fragile commodity. Once broken, it is difficult to reconnect. My dad used to say, "You can never un-ring a bell." Effective leaders know to work hard to build and maintain trust by being trustworthy.

- ➢ Effective leaders know they should not be governed by their emotions or feelings, but rather operate from principle-based behaviors, regardless of their situations.

- ➢ Because of principle-based convictions, effective leaders know to discipline their actions with responsible responses rather than reacting from inappropriate feelings.

- ➢ Effective leaders know intimidation and fear always precede defeat.

➤ Effective leaders know they need to keep their tempers and bad attitudes, because no one else wants them.

➤ Effective leaders know creditable and sustainable change in leadership must be principle-based.

➤ Effective leaders own the fact that they are responsible for the culture displayed among followers within their organizations.

➤ Effective leaders know when they make a commitment, they build hope. They also know when they keep their commitment, they build trust.

➤ Effective leaders know and understand their followers are a direct reflection of what they see as values and norms from the leader, both good and bad. Therefore, the leaders must model what they expect to see.

➤ Effective leaders know they must not only lean into their gifts and strengths, but also maintain a focus on demonstrating good character.

➤ Effective leaders know even a broken clock will be right twice daily, so the leader trusts but verifies.

- ➢ Effective leaders know they must align themselves with individuals who possess competence and outstanding character.

- ➢ Effective leaders know that people don't choose their passions, but instead their passions choose them.

- ➢ Effective leaders know, while being liked is important, being trusted and respected are foundational leadership characteristics.

- ➢ Effective leaders know integrity is a foundational trait for all leaders.

Adaptabilty

7

Being emotionally intelligent is a key. Effective leaders must deal with ambiguity and changing situations confidently and cross-culturally.

➢ Effective leaders think short and long-term. They know patience is a virtue, so they engage in well-thought-out processes and trust them for results, making adjustments as needed.

➢ Effective leaders know to resist normal temptation to surround themselves with others who are just like them. They embrace diversity so they can see and operate from a 360-degree point of view.

➢ Effective leaders know the value of pivoting. When unexpected circumstances arise, they know to pause and pivot in order to adjust resources or plans to move forward toward their mission.

➢ Effective leaders know no two situations are the same; therefore, a cookie-cutter approach can be out of order. They allow principles and best practices to guide them rather than a process.

➢ Effective leaders know who they are; they intentionally gather around others who fill the gaps.

➤ Effective leaders agree with Brandon Steiner, founder and CEO of the Steiner Agency, who said, "If you want a rainbow, you gotta deal with the rain."

➤ Effective leaders know and agree with author Mac Anderson's book-title statement: *You Can't Send A Duck to Eagle School*. Both will become frustrated.

➤ Effective leaders know to always have backups, including for themselves. As my dad used to say: "One monkey don't stop no show." Effective leaders always build a great bench because stuff happens!

➤ Effective leaders know every follower is not good at everything, so they define who is responsible for what to achieve the best alignment and execution.

➤ In all situations, effective leaders know to *respond* rather than react.

➤ Because of changing landscapes and people, effective leaders know approaches that worked in the past might not work currently or in future situations.

➤ Differently from managers, effective leaders know they cannot always implement a mapped-out plan. They sometimes have to fire, then aim.

➤ Effective leaders know operating in a world of ambiguity is the norm.

➤ Effective leaders know yesterday's leadership success does not secure today's success.

➤ Effective leaders know that persistence is a learned habit, and so is quitting.

➤ Effective leaders create and build bridges across diverse individuals and groups.

➤ Effective leaders know the difference between being reactive and proactive. They don't get so busy with damage control they forget the maintenance.

➤ Effective leaders know their leadership needs to be situational. Different situations require different types of approaches to make positive differences.

➤ Effective leaders know nothing is constant except change. Therefore, they must be vigilant in keeping a finger on the pulse of internal and external dynamics to adjust and adapt in order to remain relevant and impactful. The ATA approach: Acknowledge, Trust, Adjust.

- Effective leaders know each day is a new day so they must often be willing to change or work out of their comfort zones to achieve results.

- Effective leaders know they must take care of themselves first in order to be effective in taking care of others.

- Effective leaders know the value of having a backup. In team environments, each person has a role; however, they know the support of others improves performance and morale.

- Effective leaders know they must practice resilience to be successful. There is no such thing as failure unless the leader stops.

- Effective leaders know good team players are adaptable, supportive, and collaborative.

- Effective leaders know the value of understanding their landscape, environments, and markets. Therefore, they explore what's happening by observing and listening in order to be more effective.

Empathy

8

Active listening and humility will boost morale and performance.

> ➤ Effective leaders know the importance of empathy. They know followers don't care how much you know until they know how much you care.

> ➤ Effective leaders know they perform best in areas that play to their strengths; however, they also know they need to flex, change, and adapt to situations in order to be successful.

> ➤ Effective leaders know to respect everyone and fear no one.

> ➤ Many people spend their time; however, effective leaders *invest* their time.

> ➤ Effective leaders tap into the power of their groups by seeing each person and realizing the sum of each part makes the whole complete and more stable.

> ➤ Effective leaders know to be self-aware, purpose-driven, and real.

> ➤ Effective leaders are aware that tendencies toward envy, jealousy, acting on delusional beliefs, close-minded judgment about people, and reacting to fear by losing control are all

quicksand relative to their careers and positive living in general.

➢ Effective leaders align with French philosopher Simone Weil's admonition: "Attention is the rarest and purest form of generosity."

➢ Regarding decision-making, effective leaders know to consider the input of all who would be affected by the choices made.

➢ Effective leaders have not only high IQs (intelligent quotients), but also high EQs (emotional quotients).

➢ Effective leaders embrace the Zulu greeting: *Sawubona*, meaning "I see you." More than words of politeness, it carries the importance of recognizing the worth and dignity of each person.

➢ Effective leaders know an angry outburst has a high tendency to erode loyalty and trust. Thus self-control is the prescription for such occasions.

➢ Effective leaders know it takes work to empathize with others when the leader hasn't walked in the followers' shoes.

➤ Effective leaders spend time with their followers since they know that understanding followers helps with empathy.

➤ Contrary to common tendencies, effective leaders know they must work on their compassion and patience with others even if they have walked in some follower's shoes.

➤ Effective leaders know they need a personal board of directors to help them stay grounded as they lead, so as not to be out of touch (i.e., seeking feedback, demanding privileges, walking the talk, admitting mistakes, sharing spotlight, and so on).

➤ Effective leaders know the value of having an executive coach, or at least a mentor.

➤ Effective leaders know to avoid the everyday leadership potholes of using positional power motivated by ego or self-interest.

➤ Effective leaders know how to connect with followers using the three Fs: Feel, Felt, and Found. These words help them relate empathetically with others.

➢ To increase empathy, effective leaders know to daily practice habit number five in Stephen Covey's book, *The 7 Habits of Highly Effective People*: "Seek first to understand, then to be understood."

Continuous Learning

Ongoing seeking and acquiring new skills and best practices to be relevant.

➤ Effective leaders know they should listen to and align with the admonition of P. T. Barnum: "Money is a terrible master but an excellent servant."

➤ While pouring into others is important, effective leaders know they must invest in themselves also.

➤ Effective leaders know not to let others own them. While advisors, mentors, and close confidants can have tremendous value, effective leaders avoid allowing themselves to be put in positions of obligation by taking more than they give.

➤ Effective leaders know time is their most precious commodity, so they use it wisely.

➤ Effective leaders focus on transformation of followers.

➤ Effective leaders know their followers must know what success looks like and care about achieving it.

➤ Effective leaders agree with Julie Zhuo's ideas from her book *The Making of a Manager*. They constantly ask themselves how they can ensure purpose, people, and processes are in synch so that targeted results will be achieved.

➤ Effective leaders help followers play to their strengths.

➤ Effective leaders refuse to live below their potential.

➤ Because effective leaders are ongoing learners, they seek and value continual feedback from their followers for best alignment relative to targeted outcomes.

➤ Effective leaders know how to take care of themselves and others by being self-disciplined and set boundaries.

➤ Effective leaders know they often need to be twice as good as their competition to be considered just as good.

➤ Effective leaders know the value of having a coach. Many often use their managers for this role or hire a professional coach.

- Effective leaders know the value of having mentors and strive to make mentors of everyone.

- Effective leaders know they must be continual learners, so they take advantage of formal training in the form of seminars, conferences, workshops, and so forth.

- Effective leaders know in order to grow their followers they must effectively delegate to them.

- Effective leaders know the basic purpose of leadership is to create other leaders, so they work to put themselves out of a job.

- While leadership can take on many forms, effective leaders know the ultimate goal is transformation of followers.

- The concept of situational leadership was introduced to us by Ken Blanchard. Effective leaders know they must meet each person where they are before attempting to transform them to where the leader desires them to be.

- Effective leaders know crises present themselves with two sides. The Chinese use two brushstrokes to write the word *crisis*. One brush stoke stands for the word *danger* and the other for *opportunity*.

➤ When faced with conflict and/or adversity, effective leaders know the situations are teachable moments, realizing sometimes you lose, but you always have the opportunity to learn and grow.

➤ While intellectual understanding has value, effective leaders know real leadership is learned and perfected by doing and being in the game to gain experience.

➤ Effective leaders know that to become effective, they must do effective leadership work—no shortcuts!

➤ Effective leaders know growth is a continual process. The more the leader becomes self-aware, purpose-driven, and real, the more experience and therefore influence are gained.

➤ Effective leaders know they can only grow when exposed and challenged by new situations that produce results.

➤ Effective leaders know they need to have a mentor or coach to help them navigate their current and future landscapes.

➤ Effective leaders' thinking is based on past experiences. To help change thinking, they must challenge themselves with different experiences to achieve different and effective outcomes.

➤ Effective leaders know they should never stop learning since life never stops teaching.

➤ Effective leaders are constant and consistent learners.

➤ Effective leaders know they must take calculated risks to achieve their vision; however, they are aware that not all risks will produce desired outcomes. They are prepared for the point John Maxwell highlighted in the title of one of his books, *Sometimes You Win and Sometimes You Learn.*

➤ Effective leaders lean into Plato's position from centuries ago that you learn more about a person in an hour of play than from a year of conversation.

➤ Effective leaders know to apply discipline to gain knowledge needed to make smart decisions, convert knowledge into action, and ensure accountability for themselves and followers.

➤ Effective leaders know the majority of people struggle with change; however, they understand growth does not happen without change.

➢ Effective leaders know they are not islands; therefore, they intentionally build personal boards of directors.

➢ Effective leaders know that setbacks are just setups for better comebacks.

➢ Effective leaders know if they are not moving forward they are going backward.

➢ Effective leaders know they must be perpetual learners. Leadership is a journey, not a destination.

➢ Effective leaders know attitude is everything. Leadership guru John C. Maxwell said it best: "Attitude can be our best friend or worst enemy, the librarian of our past, the speaker of our present and the prophet of our future."

➢ Effective leaders know getting ongoing constructive feedback is critical to move out of their comfort zones.

➢ Effective leaders know they must manage their *gifts* of time daily.

➢ Effective leaders know not to embrace an "if it ain't broke, don't fix it" mindset. Rather, they embrace continual improvement.

➢ Effective leaders know they do not have all the answers; therefore, they employee brainstorming without boundaries to move the needle.

➢ Effective leaders know Rome was not built in a day; therefore, successful habits can't be built that way either.

NOTES

NOTES

NOTES

NOTES

NOTES

NOTES

NOTES

Printed in the United States
by Baker & Taylor Publisher Services